Birthday

&

Nobody

Two Plays by
Crystal Skillman

A Samuel French Acting Edition

New York Hollywood London Toronto

SAMUELFRENCH.COM

Copyright © 2011 by Crystal Skillman

ALL RIGHTS RESERVED

Cover Photo by Daniel Talbott
Pictured on the cover: Molly Ward and MacLeod Andrews

CAUTION: Professionals and amateurs are hereby warned that *BIRTHDAY & NOBODY* is subject to a licensing fee. It is fully protected under the copyright laws of the United States of America, the British Commonwealth, including Canada, and all other countries of the Copyright Union. All rights, including professional, amateur, motion picture, recitation, lecturing, public reading, radio broadcasting, television and the rights of translation into foreign languages are strictly reserved. In its present form the play is dedicated to the reading public only.

The amateur and professional live stage performance rights to *BIRTHDAY & NOBODY* are controlled exclusively by Samuel French, Inc., and licensing arrangements and performance licenses must be secured well in advance of presentation. PLEASE NOTE that amateur licensing fees are set upon application in accordance with your producing circumstances. When applying for a licensing quotation and a performance license please give us the number of performances intended, dates of production, your seating capacity and admission fee. Licensing fees are payable one week before the opening performance of the play to Samuel French, Inc., at 45 W. 25th Street, New York, NY 10010.

Licensing fee of the required amount must be paid whether the play is presented for charity or gain and whether or not admission is charged.

Professional/Stock licensing fees quoted upon application to Samuel French, Inc.

For all other rights than those stipulated above, apply to: Samuel French, Inc., at 45 W. 25th Street, New York, NY 10010.

Particular emphasis is laid on the question of amateur or professional readings, permission and terms for which must be secured in writing from Samuel French, Inc.

Copying from this book in whole or in part is strictly forbidden by law, and the right of performance is not transferable.

Whenever the play is produced the following notice must appear on all programs, printing and advertising for the play: "Produced by special arrangement with Samuel French, Inc."

Due authorship credit must be given on all programs, printing and advertising for the play.

ISBN 978-0-573-69957-3   Printed in U.S.A.   #29912

No one shall commit or authorize any act or omission by which the copyright of, or the right to copyright, this play may be impaired.

No one shall make any changes in this play for the purpose of production.

Publication of this play does not imply availability for performance. Both amateurs and professionals considering a production are strongly advised in their own interests to apply to Samuel French, Inc., for written permission before starting rehearsals, advertising, or booking a theatre.

No part of this book may be reproduced, stored in a retrieval system, or transmitted in any form, by any means, now known or yet to be invented, including mechanical, electronic, photocopying, recording, videotaping, or otherwise, without the prior written permission of the publisher.

MUSIC USE NOTE

Licensees are solely responsible for obtaining formal written permission from copyright owners to use copyrighted music in the performance of this play and are strongly cautioned to do so. If no such permission is obtained by the licensee, then the licensee must use only original music that the licensee owns and controls. Licensees are solely responsible and liable for all music clearances and shall indemnify the copyright owners of the play and their licensing agent, Samuel French, Inc., against any costs, expenses, losses and liabilities arising from the use of music by licensees.

IMPORTANT BILLING AND CREDIT REQUIREMENTS

All producers of *BIRTHDAY & NOBODY must* give credit to the Author of the Play in all programs distributed in connection with performances of the Play, and in all instances in which the title of the Play appears for the purposes of advertising, publicizing or otherwise exploiting the Play and/or a production. The name of the Author *must* appear on a separate line on which no other name appears, immediately following the title and *must* appear in size of type not less than fifty percent of the size of the title type.

BIRTHDAY was first presented by Rising Phoenix Rep (Daniel Talbott, Artistic Director) April 2, 2009 at Seventh Street Small Stage at Jimmy's No. 43, New York City. It was directed by Daniel Talbott. The cast was as follows:

LEILA	Julie Kline
KYLE	Denis Butkus

BIRTHDAY received it's U.K. premiere on August 10, 2010 at Waterloo East Theatre (Gerald Armin, Artistic Director) in it's Best of Festivals (Dominic Lindesay-Bethune, producer). It was directed by Sharon Willems. The cast was as follows:

LEILA	Katy Federman
KYLE	Andrew Glen

NOBODY was first presented by Rising Phoenix Rep (Daniel Talbott, Artistic Director) February 19, 2009 at Seventh Street Small Stage at Jimmy's No. 43, New York City. It was directed by Daniel Talbott. The cast was as follows:

KAT	Jessica Dickey
ALEX	Haynes Thigpen
KASH	MacLeod Andrews
ILONA	Polly Lee
LOUISE	Kathryn Kates
ANNA	Molly Ward

FOREWARD

Whenever I walk down East 7th street towards the Small Stage theatre at 2nd Avenue and Jimmy's, I think of Crystal. That's really not an exaggeration–she always pops into my head and is with me when I make the walk there, and I love it. That hyper-real, claustrophobic, backroom bar space is such a homebase for all of us at Rising Phoenix and for everybody that we've ever gotten to work with there, but Crystal was the first, and her openness, fearlessness and extraordinary love of adventure is one of the first memories I have of Jimmy's. I can't even begin to say how thankful I am for that.

I remember calling Crystal when we lived a few blocks from each other in Boerum Hill, Brooklyn and asking her what she was up to and if she wanted to take a walk with me. It was an early fall night and we walked up Dean Street towards Court and talked about theatre, ghosts, urban folk tales, and the occult, and I asked her if she wanted to write a play for Jimmy's or The Seventh Street Small Stage. She said yes, and a few weeks later we started rehearsal on her play *The Telling*. It's now 2011, and we've gotten to work on five plays together at Jimmy's, including the plays in this collection, and she's not only one of my closest friends and collaborators but also someone who I've grown up with as a theatre artist–I've stood behind her and she's stood behind me. Jimmy's has an extraordinary way of doing that for you, both personally and in the work. It forces you to reach out, to get honest without losing a sense of theatre and imagination, and it doesn't ever allow you to drop back and play it safe.

I love Crystal's enormous and explosive imagination paired with her deep deep love of the theatre, and these two beautiful plays, *Birthday* and *Nobody*, are such wonderful examples of both. Jimmy's is such a great foundation for anybody working in the theatre, and with Crystal it forces her to bring all of that gorgeous theatrical madness (in the best sense of the word) to the table and then ground it in relationship and honesty. I actually can't remember exactly why or what the impetus was to start writing both *Nobody* and *Birthday*, or if she ever really told me, all I know is that I feel so lucky to have gotten to work with her and all of those stunning and incredible folks on both of them, and that getting to do them back to back was insanely special and enlightening. Getting to experience the diversity of the worlds, language, and beauty of both plays next to each other is something I'll never forget.

I really hope if you're reading this that you're getting to work on both *Nobody* and *Birthday*, or one or the other, and that you're getting the chance to enter into Crystal's beautifully skewed and huge hearted world. She is a person and playwright who believes in the power of theatre and of love, and I think we would all live in a much better and more wonderfully wacky and supportive place if we could move through the world like her and her writing.

– Daniel Talbott
Director, *Birthday* and *Nobody*

INTRODUCTION

For me, directing *Birthday* was like slow dancing with a new love for the first time. I was full of hope and excitement, and sometimes fear, yes, but despite this I wanted to take my time and enjoy the dance. Likewise, I wanted my production to affect the audience with the same truth and tenderness I felt when I first read *Birthday*. More than anything, I didn't want the audience to feel like they were just sitting in a black box politely seeing a play any more than I wanted my actors to feel they were simply performing them. The challenge for me was to gently guide my actors and the audience to feel like they were really in the play together. Sounds simple, doesn't it?

In truth, the rehearsal process was a search for simplicity. I fought the urge to overcomplicate things with fancy staging or design. In some ways the story is so familiar, two strangers meeting by chance, each with a secret that is revealed by the curtain's fall. But this is only the beginning of the story. There's so much going on with each of these people: questions of love and regret and disappointment and hope. Big things. To really free ourselves to dance, we had to look at the basics of how these characters share the space and how we share it with the audience. Through solving this, I felt we could really begin to bring the world to life.

For our production, it was important for us to establish the back room as Kyle's space from the onset. We exposed the theatre's brick walls and included artefacts from his life everywhere, cds, a book of Bukowski poetry, a guitar in the corner, photos half-hung up. When we later learn that this isn't just the back room of any bar, but Kyle's place, it's as if the audience is told a secret they already know. A big part of subtly deteriorating the constructed separation of spectator and performer came from including them in moments like these. Like Leila, we invited the audience to look at the space with fresh eyes.

By giving Kyle control of the space, we began an unspoken game of permission and acceptance. As he accepted Leila and began to open the space to her, my hope was the audience would feel accepted as well. In rehearsal we found that both Andrew and Katy were naturally drawn to certain parts of the room, and as we staged the piece, these spots were like safety blankets for the characters. We toyed with which moments felt appropriate to leave them and allow the safety zones to evolve and overlap. This way the room could continue to have a life and not simply be a stage in a theatre.

By the end of *Birthday,* all of the space was a safe haven for each character equally. As we worked, I began to envision it almost like a circle. Nothing existed inside but these two people, the audience and our honesty with each other. For the final image of Leila and Kyle with the candle, I knew I wanted us all to see nothing but these two people saving each other. One of our mantras throughout rehearsal and performance was 'Be in the room.' It's so simple, but sometimes it's those simple things that prove most effective.

Directing *Birthday* was a beautiful time for me. The joy of working with Crystal's beautiful text and my actors was an amazing gift, and I hope your time with the play is just as rewarding. As you read *Birthday* and begin to imagine your own world for Leila and Kyle, I encourage you to trust your instincts, have fun, and remember to dance.

– Sharon Willems
Director, *Birthday* (UK Premiere)

ACKNOWLEDGEMENTS

To Daniel Talbott whose direction taught me so much and who always pushed me and my work in all the right ways, to all the Rising Phoenix Rep actors who always made the work the best it could be, to Jimmy who gave us a home (and beer!), to Sharon Willems and her wonderful actors who staged the production in London and made my first trip there truly magical, to my husband Fred who loves and believes in me and makes sure I always know this is true, to my mom and dad and their crazy idea to encourage anything I wanted to do, to anyone passing by the front desk while I wrote these plays, to those who came to see these plays, to those that will stage and read and see them next – thank you.

-Crystal Skillman

TABLE OF CONTENTS

BIRTHDAY 11
NOBODY..35

BIRTHDAY

CHARACTERS
LEILA - 29
KYLE - 31

SETTING
A bar

TIME
Now, spring.

(The back room of a local bar.)

(Boxing poster in the corner, memorabilia hangs on the orange walls.)

(The sounds of a party in the next room bleeds through.)

(Loud music, laugher, a girl squealing.)

*(**KYLE** drinks alone in the corner of the room, listening to a album like Neil Young's* Harvest, *which is playing on his iPhone, plugged into the backroom speakers.*)*

*(**LEILA**, upset, enters abruptly, holding her beer awkwardly.)*

(She's clearly been crying.)

*(She sees **KYLE**, turns away.)*

(breathes heavily)

(uses some toilet paper from her pocket or in her hands to blow her nose, wipe her eyes)

*(**KYLE**, who's been watching, shifts uncomfortably, turns down music, tries to say something.)*

KYLE. Can I help you?

LEILA. I'm sorry.

    I'm sorry.

    You don't have to –

    I'm sorry.

    Oh my god I must look like a fucking idiot.

(Loud laughter bleeds through the walls from the party in the next room.)

---

*Please see Music Use Note on Page 3.

LEILA. *(cont.)* They sound like an earthquake. Don't they?
Erupting.

I mean volcano.

Earthquakes are silent.

Brokers, so any chance to celebrate.
They took their ties off.
Shirts all hanging out.
Sweating.
I mean, they're seriously…

This is embarrassing, but I can't stop —

KYLE. Should I leave?

LEILA. No I'm fine, stay, stay.
You were here.

(looking for a place to throw out her tissue)

Is there a…?

KYLE. Oh if you go back - back around.

(He gestures to a little alcove offstage where the garbage can is. **LEILA** *follows his directions, disappears for a second.)*

LEILA. *(off)* Is there a light?

KYLE. Yeah to the right.

LEILA. *(off)* Thank you.

*(***LEILA** *comes back out.)*

Do you mind telling me…?
My makeup? I must look…

KYLE. Fine.

*(***LEILA** *gives him a look.)*

LEILA. Great really means okay.
Good means you've got gunk somewhere.
Fine means you look like shit.

KYLE. You look great.

LEILA. Yeah.
Leila.

KYLE. Kyle.

LEILA. Hi.

KYLE. Hi.

LEILA. What?

KYLE. Leila. You don't hear it often.

LEILA. Seventies parents.

You know that Simon & Garfunkel song about the boxer.

"I am just a poor boy though my story's seldom told" yadayadayada.

They go in the chorus, "Li, Li, Li"

There was this friend I had in middle school, big fan, went nuts – kept saying, "They're not saying your name, they're just going Li, li, li."

But I don't know, I believed it.

I like that song.

It's a depressing fucking song but, uh, I like it.

My last name is Wood.

Leila Wood.

So there goes pretty.

(**LEILA** *looks at the wall, where noise from the party keeps seeping in.*)

It's so packed – it's so full – no one can hear what you're saying.

You're like an ant.

There's been all these birthday parties.

Everyone's born in the spring I guess.

KYLE. I guess.

LEILA. It's dark back here.

KYLE. It's a good place. To just be...

LEILA. They're like kids when they go out.

"What did you do last night?"

"What movie did you see?"

"Who got laid where?"

Just dumb, boring-ass shit.

(beat)

LEILA. *(cont.)* When I'm at the front desk it's like I'm on a stage.

Everyone's passing by you to get in and out.

I don't know why I came.
The way they talk, makes my headache.

KYLE. People like them. Birthday parties.

LEILA. It's prehistoric.

The cake, candles.

People singing.

Presents.

KYLE. "The world doesn't encounter us until we meet it alone."

LEILA. *(pointing to him)* Writer.

KYLE. No. Heard it somewhere.

(They drink.)

*(***KYLE*** drinks more.)*

LEILA. You like your stout.

I never know what to get here - I just got mine because of the name.

Old Speckled Hen.

I think because I'm obsessed with farms.

All that driving through fields and passing barns all the time when I was a kid.

I did 4-H and all that, and I was, I was shit at it.

Animals kinda hate me actually, I think.

I was like in high school coming back from some Thanksgiving thing with my parents - and there was this horse in the middle of the road.
No one else around.

And instead of, I don't know calling someone, my mom gets like, "We've got to help it."
This horse is like a baby elephant.

Huge to me.

Somehow my mom's shrill voice (which would probably make me run into ongoing traffic) seems to be coxing the horse over to the park.

I'm just following behind, my head low like please God don't let anybody see my stupid-ass mom talking to a horse on Sheafe Road.

But we do get him off the road.

It's like a miracle.

It worked.

And then I'm like, you know I feel something for this horse we saved, his eyes are like gleaming and it seems like there's a connection, you know?

And I want to touch him.

I take like one step and he rears up.

It's like unreal - the setting sun behind - blinding off the snow - and thank god I totally remembered how in Ghandi Ben Kinsley threw his boney ass to the ground to save everyone from these charging horses.

And it works – the horse settles, trots toward the barn.

When we get home and I go the bathroom and I don't know how but somehow when it raised up, the horse totally grazed me and so there's like a cut on…

(motions to her breast)

I mean I'm like kill me now.

I tell my mom and then she's calling the doctor and like,

"Yes, I know it's Thanksgiving but I'm calling because my daughter got bitten on her breast by a horse."

And later I thought, of course this happened.

Because any time you try too hard. Reach out. Help. This is what happens. You get –

Yeah, I'm telling you. All the good stuff. Classic tit chomping horse stories.

LEILA. *(cont)* Christ - do you know that I recount my life to homeless people on the street. I go to the tops of towers and scream out my life.

MTA guys.

Waitresses.

Cab drivers they try to tell me their shit but I cut them off and tell them what happened to me.

Fuck…

I'm going to shut up. I'm shutting up now.

(beat)

I should.

I really should –
You see all the decorations?
My decorations?
When they sent me out to get shit they had specific requests.
Like little fucking flowers and happy faces.
Pink and yellow balloons.
A Happy Birthday banner.
In Duane Reade staring at aisles of this stuff.
"What would Joan like?"

KYLE. She's a friend of yours?

LEILA. I'd like to tell you she's a quiet girl.
I mean shy and…like a spinster in one of those movies.
Like sewing and waiting.
Like the Heiress and it's raining and she runs out to meet him even though everyone's like – wait – your big dress is going to get rained on and she goes out and looks like shit but he doesn't care and then – well it's spring so she has a shitload of kids.

KYLE. You don't know her.

LEILA. The truth is Joan is big and fat and eats all the bagels on bagel Fridays.

KYLE. Good for her.

LEILA. Why?

KYLE. I mean you come to a bar for what?

To celebrate or drown your mistakes.

Forget.

LEILA. I can't forget anything.

You come here a lot?

KYLE. I haven't been here in a while.

I'm going back tonight.

LEILA. Where?

KYLE. California.

LEILA. Just a short trip.

KYLE. Right.

(Beat. They listen to the music.)

LEILA. I love this song.

I write songs.

KYLE. Yeah?

LEILA. They're stupid, silly songs. I make them up at the front desk.

(beat)

It was my dad's fault – got me into it – got me the guitar.

On one of my birthdays, actually.

Made me keep my eyes closed, drove up to the strip mall.

And I'm getting kind of excited.

Thinking of the possibilities.

I open my eyes and there's Dunkin' Donuts.

And he's like not there.

Points next door to Mike's Music Orama.

I'd never asked for one.

Didn't want to play.

It was kinda horrible really because then I had to take all these lessons.

I would make my teachers cry because I never practiced.

KYLE. I played drums in high school.

LEILA. No shit.

KYLE. *(name of band:)* The Skinny Dicks.

> *(raises glass to her)*
>
> High school.
>
> *(She laughs.)*

LEILA. High School.

> *(They laugh.)*
>
> *(They drink.)*
>
> Where did you go to college?

KYLE. Where didn't I go?

LEILA. Sarah Lawrence. Scholarship.

> *(She toasts him back.)*
>
> What do you do now?

KYLE. I don't know.
Anything.
Nothing.
It doesn't matter.

LEILA. You're married.

KYLE. Yeah.

> *(beat)*

LEILA. You want to hear something real stupid?
I can remember like all these old birthdays my mom threw.
The cakes, my dresses.
I make fun of it but I used to take it really seriously.
My wishes.
I really closed my eyes.
Like I really believed…

KYLE. Only child.

LEILA. How do you know?

KYLE. I wasn't.

LEILA. How many?

KYLE. Two brothers, one sister.

LEILA. You're close?

KYLE. We're family.

LEILA. My folks call me at the front desk all the time.

They ask me so many questions, most I can't answer, as if I know what's going to happen.

"Do you think they're ever gonna hire you for real?"
"What do you think you're gonna to do next?"
"Do you think you're gonna meet someone?"

"Where are the babies??"

They didn't call today.

(KYLE drinks. LEILA studies him.)

I don't want you to feel bad for me.

(Beat.)

Do you know that an old, old man – like white hair, nice looking guy but old – like 93 years old comes up to me real close in midtown.

"Me no speak English."

I think he's going to ask for like directions to Macy's. But he leans in and if he wasn't so old maybe I'd be worried but as it is he's so old I could breath and he'd fall over.

He leans in:

"Me looking for sex."

I'm just standing there, trying to figure out where to go for lunch you know.

And my first reaction is to laugh, but for some reason I don't want to offend him.

So I tell him, "Not me. But many others."

And his eyes, he got so excited – looking up and down the street full of so many possibilities.

Like a kid in a candy store.

And I didn't know what to do.

We shook hands, I left.

KYLE. Okay.

LEILA. Strangers ask for directions, sex apparently all the time, but…

I don't know.

It's not often you meet someone, who would take the time…

Take the time to…

I don't know.

KYLE. This city can be great that way.

LEILA. It's just I see someone like you and I wish I was. More…

KYLE. More?

LEILA. I don't know.

Together?

(beat)

I bet she's opening the presents now.

KYLE. Joan.

LEILA. Joan.

Bet they're funny stuff, like fake post its.

You put them places, they say like, "Meet me at the Water Cooler," you know.

It's crazy. Giving this crap.

I still remember some Pretty Pink Pony thing that I got – Rainbow Star.

If you can believe it.

My friend in 7th grade made her into a bong.

Could take off the head, a little pipe in the body, water in the legs.

It was probably toxic but we smoked the shit out of Rainbow Star.

We smoked her in the JC Penney parking lot.

KYLE. I was always obsessed with comics but my parents always bought me cars.

LEILA. You like comics?

Guys like jerk off to those things – like all over Wonder Woman's tits.

KYLE. That's a myth. Seriously. Graphic novels are an art form.

LEILA. I guess that's why that guy was spouging in the Virgin Megastore.

KYLE. No.

LEILA. He was defiantly ogling.

KYLE. Isn't it the same thing? Women reading erotic mysteries on the plane?

LEILA. No.

No.

KYLE. It isn't?

LEILA. No.

KYLE. *(reciting titles:)* Desire In The Grass?

Find Me In the Shade.

Promise of Passion Paradise.

LEILA. You seem to know a lot about middle age female erotica.

KYLE. I fly a lot.

LEILA. You and Joan could trade titles.

KYLE. I think she's got more experience than me.

LEILA. Poor Joan.

(They smile.)

She's been there for years.

She knows where everything is.

What everyone wants.

I've only been there a year.

I'm a temp.

Just a temp.

Saying it I feel like…

It's just getting older - you expect things to start to make sense.

(beat)

Where's your wife?

KYLE. Anguilla.

LEILA. I don't even know where that is.

(She laughs.)

(They drink.)

KYLE. It's all…the same.
Beaches, boats, cars.

LEILA. That's where you live.

KYLE. That's where we stay. Sometimes. Her mother's there.

LEILA. Everyone at work talks about going scuba diving or skiing. Sometimes they send their pictures out to the whole staff.

One guy, sent like a million – at the end there's this picture of him underwater in his little banana hammock just…waving at the camera.

It was, it was embarrassing. —And then to see him after, in the hall.

You don't get that out of your head.

KYLE. I imagine not.

LEILA. I don't do any of that. I don't do anything.

KYLE. Just write songs.

(She bows.)

What did you study?

LEILA. What didn't I study?

(He smiles.)

But I settled on English lit.

KYLE. I wanted to be a chef. Well, first an architect, then a chef.

*(**LEILA** smiles.)*

Jesus, that sounds.

LEILA. No, it doesn't.

KYLE. Yeah, it does, but it's true.

My family thought I was crazy. When I told them I wanted to buy this place, you should have seen my dad.

He was like stuttering it out: A b-b-bar?

It's like falling in love.
Like I'm here.
Put on my music.
I can just listen.

LEILA. To crazy nuts like me.

KYLE. To all sorts of things.

LEILA. Like broker boys going insane.

(Beat, then she can't contain herself:)

Oh my god, you own this place?

KYLE. Yeah, it's a little weird.

LEILA. *(Smiling – like "wow")* It's fucking insane.

(Beat.)

I bet they're whacking the piñata.
Yeah, they asked for one.
They didn't have any birthday ones so I found one in the Easter aisle.
It's like an egg.
They're beating a giant crepe paper egg.

My mom – she used to dress up like the Easter Bunny.
The Lucky Charms lady on St. Patty's Day.
I'm not shitting you.
Our house was holiday central.

KYLE. We don't do anything like that.

LEILA. You're lucky. It makes things easier. No expectations.

KYLE. What do you expect?

LEILA. What do you mean?

KYLE. I don't know.

LEILA. Oh god. It'll make you sick.
It's just like fantasy.

KYLE. So.

LEILA. It's typical Good Living Martha Stewart Magazine layout shit.

LEILA. *(cont)* The house.
>Kids.
>Like an unrealistic amount of kids I don't even want.
>Lots of animals.
>Dogs, cats, turtles, ferrets, the whole thing.

KYLE. *(smiling)* Sounds reasonable I –

>*(Holds up her hand. More to come:)*

LEILA. A backyard.
>A tree house.
>Next door neighbors.
>And even though this seems out of the city.
>It's in the city.
>Next to all the buildings, just a few trees on the street.
>Tire swing.
>A shitload of flowers.
>Grass.
>Someone to help clean and take care of things.
>A guy?
>Maybe?
>Paid enough so it's respectable.
>A fucking amazing husband.
>Who wants to go to bars and sing karoke and smoke pot once in a while.

KYLE. Out of Rainbow Star.

LEILA. No more horses. A bong would do just fine.
>And you know he could be tall.

KYLE. Like a tall, dark, bulging tit handsome guy.

LEILA. Look, you've got Wonder Woman.

KYLE. Touché.

LEILA. And Mr. Tall, dark and VERY handsome bulging tit guy and I would get married and there would be a car with a bunch of dumb-ass shit tied to it and signs.

KYLE. Sounds like a beautiful wedding.

LEILA. Has it all been what you expected?

KYLE. What?

LEILA. Being married?

KYLE. You learn to stop expecting.

(beat)

LEILA. My friend from high school, she turned born again Christian.

So she would write me letters about waking up and the devil would be at the bottom of her bed.

And when she met her husband, she prayed to God to see if they should kiss.

So there, at the wedding, when she was crying like crazy, I realized it had to be her thinking of what it would be like for the first time.

With this guy she never…

And she's scared but no one cares.

Her family was so happy.

Throwing her into the car.

With the cans and the signs, even with her crying.

They were just so happy that she was…

That she'd be taken care of.

KYLE. Was she?

LEILA. They couldn't have kids.

I didn't ask why.

But there was a part of me that wondered – maybe they just didn't figure it out.

How it all works.

Horrible, I know.

But the good news is she got a baby from China that someone wrapped in a butcher apron and left on the steps of some orphanage.

She's so into it she wants to adopt another one but ran of money so she's fundraising.

KYLE. People get…people get crazy.

LEILA. Yeah.

KYLE. When my wife got pregnant, you should have seen my mom's eyes.

To get us married.

LEILA. Girl?

KYLE. Boy.

LEILA. How old?

KYLE. Four.

LEILA. Do you have pictures?

*(**KYLE** unplugs iPhone, goes over to her, scrolls through pictures on it, showing her.)*

He's cute.

KYLE. You could say that.

(He continues to scroll.)

LEILA. Is that…your wife?
She's beautiful.

KYLE. Yeah.

She doesn't even know I'm here.

*(**KYLE** gets up, goes back to his corner, plugs the iPhone back in, the music comes back on.)*

*(Long beat: **LEILA** looks at **KYLE**. He's silent, looking down.)*

*(Then **LEILA** goes to the area where music or variety acts play in this backroom. It might be a little stage in the corner, or just an area with a microphone set up.)*

LEILA. I should have a puppet and a ukulele.

*(**KYLE** watches her, curious.)*

Don't get excited. This is not like. This is not a show.

KYLE. Um. Yes. It is.

LEILA. No.

Just a little song.

KYLE. Should I cheer like – "Li-li-li".

LEILA. Cute but please - no.

KYLE. I could do the drums.

(LEILA starts singing along to the song that's playing, softly at first, then gets into it.)

(Sings fully, beautifully free, then stops herself.)

Oh god you hate it.

KYLE. No it's. Beautiful.

LEILA. Really?

KYLE. Really. I'm impressed.

LEILA. It's new.

(beat)

In my building.
When it was snowing out of nowhere here last month.
All these seagulls fly past my windows.
Fucking weird, right?
Right in the snow.
The way they moved, right up to the windows, glide their bodies right by, then raise up, that's grace I thought.
I'd like to move like that.

Some people make mistakes but can move through them, let them go and they don't hurt.
They don't cry in hallways and look like shit.
They sit in corners and keep it all inside.
But I can't.

I have this wish, the way I want things to be.
And when I see it, in my head, it's good, it's good but how can I make that…
I dream about it.
Being that.
I wake up.
It's a feeling.
Alive like…
Like there are all these possibilities.
But I wake up.
I lose it.

KYLE. I had a…
>My friend she…
>I came out here for her funeral.
>A car accident.

>I loved her.
>I loved her very much.

>She asked me if I had the strength to change, to be with her.

>But back then I didn't. I left.

>When I was with her I was so much, thought I could be so much.

LEILA. I'm sorry.

KYLE. It's okay.

(silence)

LEILA. It's so quiet now.
>People must be leaving, getting coats.
>Joan.

KYLE. Joan.

(beat)

LEILA. At the end of my lunch hour I ran around to pick up stuff for the party.
>I stared at everything, the decorations, the pile of cakes.
>Staring at frosting and everything in me felt gone.
>Greg and I – this guy at work - for months now- it's been…something.
>I thought it was.
>That it had possibilities.
>I picked out a white cake.
>Red icing.
>Bought the candles.
>Go back.
>Open the door.

Answer the phones.

Surf the web.

And just before we're supposed to leave Greg takes me to the top, to the roof of the building.

The top of like a thousand floors.

We'd been there before.

I mean we'd go up there because at the front I have all the keys to everywhere and up there, it's like just starting to stay lighter later and we can see the sun behind everything and it's all shadows and that's like what we are too, with each other.

And we don't say shit and there's something weird about it, that makes me not want to but I can't stop that I am.

And probably like someone's looking out a window – thinking that's love or they're stupid but whatever they're thinking it's not what we are.

And after, he walks ahead of me.

Huge strides.

Ahead to the stairs to go down.

Doesn't look up to see how I am.

Doesn't look behind at all.

Just walking so fast, so far ahead of me.

Why would he do that?

At the bottom of the stairs, he tells me it's not working.

After we've…

He tells me.

After.

And I felt.

I was shaking and…

I go back in, and sit at the computer and it's like I'm not moving, I just…I can't move.

Until everyone's grabbing me and asking me "Where's the stuff for the party" and I have to come.

And I want to find a way to be happy, and I know somewhere, somehow there is a version of me that is happy.

LEILA. *(cont.)* If I can just…
Because there's no more time.
I'm 29.
It's my birthday.
And no one knows.
I didn't tell them.
There's supposed to be a list but I'm not on it.
All they know is about Joan.
All they care about is her.
And they're gathering around her.
And somewhere – there is a place with people who want to know me.
Who give a shit.
But I'm not there.
I'm here.
And drinks are everywhere and I'm downing like a fish, trying to smile.
Then the lights.
They got the waitress to turn them off and it's dark.
They start coming at Joan with the white cake with red icing.
And I close my eyes to wish, my own wish, but there's something in me so deep and so…that I wished I was…
That I could choose to…

Because I close my eyes and I don't see anything.
Ahead of me.
For me.
And I couldn't stop…

(**LEILA** *is crying.*)

(beat)

(**KYLE** *gets up.*)

(gets a candle from one of the tables)

(comes back to **LEILA***, sits next to her)*

KYLE. Didn't count.
>Never does.
>The first time.
>
>*(takes out a lighter)*
>
>*(lights the candle)*

KYLE. Close your eyes.

>**(KYLE** *looks at her, they are very close now.)*
>
>**(LEILA** *closes her eyes.)*
>
>You see it?
>You got it?
>
>**(LEILA** *nods yes.)*

KYLE. You sure?

>**(LEILA** *opens her eyes.)*

LEILA. Yes.

>**(LEILA** *blows out the candle.)*
>
>*(As she does there is the:)*
>
>*(Blackout)*

END OF PLAY

PROPERTIES

Toilet paper (to be used for tissue)
Phone
Candle

A NOTE ABOUT THE MUSIC

In the New York production, Kyle listened to his music on an iPhone that was plugged into the backroom speakers, which could be heard by the audience, allowing Leila to sing along with the album later. In London, when Leila goes to the "stage" area, there was a guitar that allowed her to sing while Kyle played. Another possiblity is using a boombox. Each production should feel free to do what works best for them.

NOBODY

CHARACTERS

KAT - Proofreader
ALEX - Chef
KASH - Beer Guy/Bartender
ILONA - Waitress
LOUISE - Widow
ANNA - Poet/Teacher

SETTING

Waiting Room.
A place for waiting.
Somewhere far away, in the dark.
Only the edges are lit.

Three years after.

TIME

Now, winter.

1. Kat is proofing, waiting by the window.

KAT. Anna had symbols and signs. Painted in black letters, spelling it out: Danger – exclamation point!

I mean right before her ceremony she fell. She didn't trip, slip, she fell down a spiral staircase in the little barn house where she was getting ready.

One of those weddings in the country you know. Three hours outside the city.

That's a sign, if you think about it. Anyone who doesn't want to get married where they are, as what they are.

Well, there's a certain level of denial, am I right?

Driving up there I was paralyzed with fear – not just because we – or I – we -.

But because I drove up and her soon to be mother-in-law was tromping across the cow field (where we're all forced to park – sedans and shit) waving her arms:

"Hello, hello! Anna's so excited to see her best friend here."

I am the fucking maid of honor for Christ's sake, it's not some kind of surprise but I assume it's the valium talking.

Anna after too much Pinot Noir – fiddling her wedding ring like crazy (another sign), letting all sorts of shit spill out:

"You know when your mother-in-law pops all these valiums from her purse" - dot, dot, dot…

Have you noticed that?

That any crazy behavior that someone wants to justify further for their own sake of mind – starts: "You know when you…"

KAT. *(cont.)* As if one's own experience would be the same thing.

As if that's what would connect us.

Her mother-in-law, still waving those long arms: "Better watch out for deer ticks up here. Check everywhere before you leave. Even your *(mouths:* vagina)."

Like I said – every sign in the world. A ticking time bomb.

But she was aware.

Just weird.
She never calls in the afternoon, like.

Even the waitress thought it was strange.
Seeing me here now.

It's been years now.
That we've been – *(Unsaid: Lovers)*.
Coming here.
Or maybe more.

Did I lose count?

Still struggling to remember her name – the waitress - kicking myself (Iona or ...?)

Gives me the vodka tonic she knew I'd ask for.

I nod, drink. Jesus, it's strong.
The backroom is practically empty. Nobody, really.
And the songs they're playing.

Mid-drink – the waitress still talking – going on. Asking what it is I do, with all the papers.

"Proofs," I say, show her the marked up pages. Deepen into my detective voice: "I collect evidence."

I realize it's what I always say to Anna.

Anna never smiled in school. She was like scowling all the time.

One night I was supposed to be finishing a paper, look out my window to see the scowling quiet girl striding past our dorm in the middle of the night.

I run down the stairs, get my coat, follow her. She goes fast - ducks into like an alleyway, jumps out, scares the shit out of me.

"Why are you following me?"

I say I don't know.

That night, that's when I learned what a secret was.

That woman who just came in, she's still wearing her coat, I don't know why, it's boiling in here by now.

It's so weird because all of it, it seems…familiar in some way.

I'm not used to waiting.

Giggling from the couple in the next room I can't see.

I don't know why Anna called. Won't tell me anything, out of breath. Says she wants to meet.

"Where?"

"Six o'clock."

After we spoke, when I put down the phone, I was exhausted, laid down, closed my eyes.

And I swear I dreamed I was here.

But I don't –

Like something exploded in me.

I remember pieces, here and there.

What if she doesn't come?

I proof.

Focus.

All symbols.

Circles.

Xs.

Red.

Did I miss what Anna was trying to tell me?

I see her at the window.

It's not her fault. I can't imagine anything more frightening than marriage.

KAT. *(cont.)* Maybe love.
> Looking at her,
> In that one moment, it all seems clear.
> It explodes in me.
> And I remember –

2. Alex faces the package in the kitchen.

ALEX. I shouldn't have gone drinking but with my old buds in town from Culinary - what was I going to do?

All we did was eat and drink, (drinking more than eating), bitch about every place, them going on about the awards they've been getting, write ups and there's a lot of turning to dear old Alex:

"What about you?"

I tell them I'm here, this place.

And they get quiet, try to act like that's respectable.
Then talk about all the women they're fucking.
How they're fucking them.

I drank more than all of them.

And even though it seems like I'm letting go, it's calculated. Me who tries to control everything, even planning in his mind where to have spontaneous sex when I get the chance.

And it pops in my mind that I haven't gotten the chance to fuck anything in three years.

When I got home, 4 in the morning, I tried to jerk off, but didn't have the heart to finish. It's like I knew what was going to happen so what's the point.

Conked out. And I know, right this sounds crazy – like how can he...?

But whatever I was dreaming I woke up.

My head feeling like a sieve at the wine store, paying for the cabernet, grigos when I don't feel any keys in my pocket, and see them – right there on the nightstand in a land far, far away.

I don't have time to go back. And my head, it's a fog.

Fucking shivering. Up to my ears in honey jars, muffins, arugula.

ALEX. *(cont.)* Walking through the market, trying to go fast because I'm late but I'm like a ghost there, walking slower and slower. I know what I want, exactly what I want, but I'm still looking over every fucking tomato.

All the time knowing I'm going to be late, nervous but suddenly strangely calm until I'm going down the stairs here.

Breaking into my own place.

I feel like a dick. I look like an asshole. And I smell like shit.

Finally the door pushes open. Dark.

It's freezing.

Turn up the heat on the way to the back, to the kitchen. At least that's working – you can feel it blasting.

Throw down the bags. Break it out: the pans I want off the wall, grab the menu board, chalk.

"Door's broken."

Kash - remarkable for noticing the obvious, comes in, throws the mail down.

He looks weirder than usual, his hair's all. Like soaking. He just looks at me, turns to escape. Grunts something, gone.

I turn to see it lying there. Yellow manila package. Big black script.

(reading how it's addressed) "To: Alexander. From ..."

From -.

When I saw, when it hit me, I couldn't breath for a moment.

Fuck it.

Take out the groceries, shallots, get the knife.

Open - the cabernet – one – fuck it - two glasses.

It's not just surprising looking at it.

It's...I don't know why.

"Alexander."

No one even calls me that anymore.

Music starts, some pop shit Ilona's obsessed with.

Getting the cutting board, I look up, catch a glimpse of myself in the huge pan hanging in front of me.

I look frightening.

"Alex."

Ilona's staring at me.

I am –. I am frightening.

I look –

"Alex."

Her voice – one of those moods.

She looks at the two glasses I've been drinking – then the package.

"What's in the envelope?"

I tell her it's linens but she knows I'm lying.

And why am I lying?

This is ridiculous, stupid I tell myself.

Five years later what do you send to a person you barely remember because I barely –

Ilona, throws the ticket at me, stomps out.

(looking at order) Two salads – fucking first date.

My reflection in the pan mirror on the wall.

But it's not just me.

It's her.

 "To: Alexander. From..."

When we first met - one of those stupid parties, could barely hear her over the music, kids coming in with drinks through the window, from the keg on the porch.

ALEX. *(cont.)* I told everyone we fucked everywhere.
Behind buildings, cars, bathrooms.
But the truth? When it was us.
It was effortless.
Like we weren't even there.

It had only been a few weeks I show her photo to my Dad.
First thing.
First thing he said: she's – she's with you?
Heard him the whole way I drove back from Jersey and when I got there, just right to bed, didn't say a thing.
She was sleeping.

Then a sound, like a whisper, sob.

She was shaking me.
Gently shaking me awake.

Asking if I…
The most basic of questions of what I had to give.
If I loved her.
As if that's all she needed.
As if after she heard that, she would be changed in some way.

And I think do I – do I really know her?

And if she – this stranger really – asks questions in the dark that you can't answer and you're supposed to. Supposed to.

I pretended to sleep, but I could hear her. I could hear her cry.
Which is funny because I didn't hear her go.

I didn't know that would be the last time –

I walked around the apartment that morning, empty.

I walked with nowhere to go.

And everyone –

Fuck them.

"How are you doing, Alex?"

Your friends.

One event doesn't make a person.

Of course no one could think I could be with her - she was *(unsaid:* Beautiful*)*.

After she left me – I did – I – I fucked everything. But wherever I was with them, I felt...I was there. My old body was there.

Something smells rotten. A stench. For a second familiar, I tell myself forget it. Kash must have left it out. Eggs. But I don't think –

(beat)

I pick the package up.

I hold it in my hands, run over the edges.

Slide the knife into it.

Air comes out, a breath.

It's my face.

I move my hands over the paint and I can feel her there.

She's written a letter too – from what I can read it's straight out of "I dumped my culinary boyfriend to go to art school 101".

Asks me to forgive her if you can believe that. For leaving without...

Has her contact info. Different last name.

Married.

It's a good painting.

I turn on the stove, start cooking.

3. Kash is jerking off in the bathroom.

KASH. Ilona, when she's cleaning glasses, she like does that thing with her eyes. It makes me so hot. Like when she puts on her lipstick, looking in the mirror. Can't even see me. Makes me so I can't stand it.

They say Kash - put the beer away and stop jerking off in there.

People get biased. It's not fair.

I keep, keep stuff in here. Hide shit everywhere to keep me company. Secrets!

(He can share the book if he has or just say:)

"Cobras - The longest poisonous snake in the world!"

The whole family made me go out to Long Island to some bogus cousin's baby shower so I got this book and my sister was like you cannot give that to a baby. I said why not. She said the baby can't read. And I said it's gonna but she said it doesn't want to read about:

"Cobras - The longest poisonous snake in the world!"

So I said fine, I'll keep it.

It says they make a nest for their eggs, stay with them.

They protect their kids.

I don't want a kid.

I don't want a dog.

I want to protect her.

Like a cobra.

People keep all sorts of crazy things as pets. Guy had a tiger in his apartment in the Heights. Shit all over the place. Open the door there, open a door like that and it's a trap.

How can I, how can I - and look at her like -

Like every day.

It's killing me, coming here every day, here and trying to just –

I'm trying.

Trying to just –

*(**KASH** comes. It's oddly silent.)*

Can't keep the water dripping down from my hair.

Salty.

It's a secret because this morning I had nothing to do, so I, I went on a bus.

Correction: I got a little high on the weed my roommate left out, ate some cheerios and outside my stoop saw all these older folks bundled up in parkas, jackets, lining up. So I said what the fuck, pulled up my coat, just walked in behind them.

It must have been some social service thing because no one even asked for money. Noticed. It's like I was someone else.

And there were extra seats. I even got one next to the window. Looked out and we were leaving the city.

Highways and trees, branches waving.

And as we went, I said goodbye to everything, and for the first time, thought maybe I knew how my brother felt when he left. Going to a new place.

Unknown.

It was like that song with the words that I don't know the lyrics to.

And maybe it was the weed, but I felt really quiet inside even though there were TVs playing game shows in the bus.

I didn't know where I was going.

I looked at all these rumpled old people – I look at them and see me. They look like spirits or something already. Something gone out of their eyes. Their faces...

KASH. *(cont.)* When I got off I was like in Atlantic City.

Ocean and bums and lots of hotels with lights on even in the day.

The old people, they just shove off. Crickety, crick.

The boardwalks, it's old, wooden, missing planks.

I see the water, walking down there.

I look out at the water, the waves, sink into the cigarette, paper cup sand. Close my eyes and it's like I'm in a seashell. Teeny, tiny.

Fell asleep. On and off, in and out, but enough to…
And I must be working too much because I dream of this place.

(His dream:) I'm in the middle of the room, everything around us is -

I turn, see Ilona.

For the first time she's looking at me.

Staring at me.

As if it could mean something.

Then - I woke up, the cold coming off the waves.

I got up and started to get a little scared. Being alone, thinking of all the shit that's happened. What you can't tell anyone.

What you'd like to tell her.

Because she's got shit she should tell you too.

Staring out, and the gulls are coming down, low. The smell of salt and breeze.

And I see something coming over the waves.

I go in – slow at first – the waves, coming up lapping. Roll up my pants, god, god – it's so cold, it's freezing but I wade in, it's going to knock me over, I'm struggling just to stand.

It's a little toy.

Green plastic.

A solider, alone.

It can barely stay afloat.

Pick it up.

And I know it's crazy but I feel like my brother, like he's –

I cry for him. I realize I haven't not really since –

I look at the solider and it looks like him.

Put it in my pocket.
Feel him there.

Barely got here in time, door just opens, no lock.

No lights.

Mail just thrown there on the steps. A package, pick it up.

For Alex who looks worse than I think I do.

I'm pulling beers when Ilona comes in.

Asking me questions.

I want to answer.

I want so badly to –

Ilona's in the back. I go behind the bar.

Leave her a secret.

Courage.

The trees at the window move in the wind, waving shadows as I walk into the middle of the room.

4. Ilona cleans the glasses at the bar.

ILONA. I am in no mood for this.

Coming in – first off it looks like the place is broken into – door wide open.

Inside: dark, silent.

No light, shit, it's...

These are all the things that tell someone to get the fuck out, like a movie when everyone's screaming get the fuck out.

And for a second something tells me:

Ilona - be careful.

I'm in no mood.

I call out.

Kash comes around the bar. Like he's been caught. Thing about Kash is he always looks guilty and for some reason his hair is like dripping wet.

I'm asking what happened to him and he just stares. Shrugs, says Alex is in the back.

So I go in, turn on the lights, taking off my coat, fixing myself. He just stands there, like always, staring.

Then disappears. And there's something about it, strange, that makes me think it's happened before. Then I'm like wake the fuck up, work.

Putting out special wines, cleaning glasses – still a little lost until the phone rings like an alarm –intrusion! - this lady asking what time we open and I'm like "now".

There's no music. I hate it when there's no music, pop in something new, and this song, I love this song like: *(imitates song)*

Looking at the shelves under the bar - that paper one of the girls has left is still there with that circled ad.

Pick it up. Been there for weeks. Audition for some soap opera thing.

I mean…really. I'd never –

But.

If I did…

I'd go in and they'd be all in a row (like on those shows) all in black shirts and jeans, very serious, designer glasses. Passionless. Ask me to read some scenes, not even listening.

And I don't know what I'm doing, but they look up, startled and I go on and they are like on the floor, it's like I'm some kind of natural.

Like star natural.

I'm not even done and they shout: "Enough!" And they sit me down slowly, as you do to someone so extraordinary - they say they want to know all about me – how I came to be - the deep down real truth that a genius creature like myself hides - my "*Days of our Lives*".

What I found out when going through my mother's dresser drawers.

Alejandro Pepe.

Twelve years old, I asked her who he was, divorce papers in hand. My mom quiet, doing that thing with her eyes, but then spills:

She was married to this rich Spanish guy but then my supposed dad, passing through on his motorcycle, just right there on the street asks her if she wants a ride (This was Arizona where apparently such things happened in the 70s.)

It must have been some ride because, as she tells it, she came back, packed, left. That was it. Until Alejandro Pepe came after them in a hotel room with a knife! Gasp! But she had him committed (which I guess you could also do in Arizona in the 70's) and moved to London.

And in my little fantasy - the producers look at each other - we must work this into your new character! And we laugh and smile and drink a fuckload of champagne.

And I could laugh about it, like it didn't mean anything.

(picks at a band-aid on her arm)

It still hurts. God, I'm a baby.

(about Kat:) She finally notices, me there with the vodka, making my rounds. Doesn't remember my name, I can tell, but I remember hers.

I look just a little bit curious – it's not when she usually comes and she's usually with…

She's waiting.

Looks small alone.

I'm asking her about all these papers she has, but she's just going on - something about evidence.

Isn't that I was looking for this morning?

The woman in that coat.
Asked what she wanted and she wouldn't say anything - just pointed to an arcane drink menu on the table. An apple-tini.

Apple-tini!

And it's weird but for a minute I feel like I know her.

The couple - kids really – old enough to be here – young enough to annoy you- in the corner, they want some of the special lager. So I call out to Kash - he answers from the bathroom. I say get the hell out of there and he says "I'm sick" and I'm like "Can you be sick faster?"

He says he's trying. To finish, whatever that means.

(feels her arm)

I just wanted them to finish up so I could get out of there this morning.

My mother didn't have to go through that – scans and needles *(gestures to arm)* and tests.

We just knew she was crazy.

("corrects" herself from before) Sorry, depressed.

So this morning when the brain guy with the accent, I call him Dr. Russia, says there's nothing he can detect – after all these weeks, not the written tests, not the physical - I'm like stunned. I find it depressing actually. Depressing that I'm not clinically depressed. Like all that for nothing. I don't know what to say so I ask him, did you find anything interesting?

He's like, "Oh it was all interesting, but all you need to know is you're fine."

"Fine."

Fuck fine.

I call another doctor. He at least gives me pills.

I go back to the kitchen, pick up the plates. Alex looks like shit, won't even talk to me, look at me, staring at the mail, won't even take the time to tell me the truth - what he's got in there.

And I just want someone to tell me the truth.

Go out, passing Kash who has emerged and is giving me some thumbs up signal like I know what that means.

And it gets so bad, what I'm feeling.

Like something is wrong with me that no one can see.

Like when I'd look at my mom and know there was some reason she shouldn't be left alone.

What would I tell my kid?

How could I have one, knowing what I know?

With all that "evidence"?

Pouring the lagers when my cell rings– my mom.

I go to the side, ringing like I'll explode.

ILONA. *(cont.)* Flip it on and I'm like I told you not to call me during work and she asks how it went this morning.

And I start bawling, I mean out of the sides so no one can see, sniffling with nowhere to wipe and I want to crawl under something and just –

She's asking me what's wrong – I can hear her asking me what's wrong.

I tell her they didn't find anything. That I'm a freak, that there's no reason for me to…

To be what? I can't finish. I'm a non reason, nobody holding two salads and a lager.

And she said, "Honey, honey – you're not me."

And I just went limp, everything went out of me. Somehow I get off the phone and I feel –

I'm spiraling past my cousins, my grandma, my uncle, all gone, all who choose to –

And it comes to me, real simple, low: I have to be something else. Someone different.

I look at the shelves under the bar, and there's this little green toy. This solider or something.

I pick it up and I don't know why but for a second I feel okay.

I hold it. I hold it so tight it's melting.

5. Louise, still wearing her coat, drinks in the corner.

LOUISE. This is, late in the evening.

It's after a show, something we've seen, dinner, drinks. We've said goodbye to our friends, made it home, exhausted.

My husband's still lingering in the bathroom light.

He says:

There's something I have to tell you.

Instantly, in my head - a thousand things. Something wrong with our son, disease, relatives, bankruptcy, another woman.

To him, I just nod, wait for him to go on, finish undressing, getting ready to go to bed like we have a hundred times before.

"It's a dream I had."

I wanted to laugh, more at myself fearing the worst.

But when he could, when he spoke again - he dreamed he saw me on a street he didn't know, had never seen.

Trees in between streets, in the middle of concrete, buildings.

The wind. Hard, rough. Pockets of ice.

I asked him, "Where are you?"

I don't know he said.

But he could see me.

I'd stopped walking.

I was turning.

Past Christmas lights strung up on the overhead of a stairway going down.

He noticed them because it was late, starting to get dark.

Three lanterns strung across the wall.

I went down until I was at the bottom, right before the wooden door, already open a crack.

LOUISE. *(cont.)* It was a pub.

He stopped talking.

It felt like a long time.

He looked up at me. I realized he hadn't been - he'd been looking down or off, not at me, not really.

You know how much I love you, he said.

He took a breath, went on. The strangers who were there. Sitting. Their faces.
He told me, how, how –
And when he finished.

To hear him, to hear him call my name.

And in this moment, this abyss after hearing that he imagined this horrible thing happening to me, there is a small eternity. A hole into which we've fallen and will never recover.

"It's just a dream."

I kiss him.

Turn out the light.

I don't sleep.

I don't dream.

(beat)

A year later, he had a heart attack in the park.

He had asked to be cremated, I watched as his body became air and bits of dust.

I had to go to another lecture – Cooper Union. I fill my time now being on committees (including committees about how to form more committees).

I didn't want to go today, so cold. But I promised someone or other I'd be there.

The lecture, lead by a professor of philosophy, a smart woman, god twenty something – it was all very good, but throughout it, I couldn't keep still.

Afterwards, we all funneled out into the street. The other ladies they – they all walked away, absorbed.

I don't go with them.

"I'm going this way," I say.

I don't know if they even heard me, as they continue on, chatting.

I walk alone.

I turn onto a street I've never seen before.

Everyone else bustling past with determination. Purpose. Going to work, coming home.

I keep walking.

The sun fading, colder.

The wind –

Headlights of cars.

Light almost gone, a dark, dark blue in the sky.

I look up – and then right in front of me –

I stop.

Everything out of me.

Thinking this can't be.

But it is.

Glowing.

Large colored bulbs casting light on the wall over the staircase.

Three lantern lights leading down.

Following the steps.

And as frightened as I am, walking in, in some way I feel alive.

The waitress looking at me and I know her face.

Because they are his words.

They are, all of them: the woman with the papers, the man with the wet hair, the waitress, –

LOUISE. *(cont.)* She greets me, looks as if she knows me.

I remember.

And I can't speak. I want to run as the door falls behind me.

I want to run but the woman with the papers stares at me, pauses from her swirls, looks up, holding her red pen.

I've stepped into it. Every word after all these years. And I can't explain it, but somehow the way they look at me, it seems they feel the same. As if…

I hear music.

A knife cutting.

Laughter.

And knowing what I know, there is another voice inside me that speaks loudly: You could go home, you could read, you could sleep, you could forget, you could dream, Louise.

But then I would never know.

And I want to know.

Stay within his words.

I pull my coat tighter.

Step inside.

Sit.

Wait.

6. Anna at the top of the stairs.

ANNA. I couldn't even move when I woke up this morning, and I was fully, I was fully awake but still dreaming about her even as my husband touches my arm as he gets up first, kisses me like he always does, a tight squeeze.

"Getting up?"

I laid there, looking out the sliding doors, second floor of our little Brooklyn Heights brownstone where the trees pop out over the front gate.

I can't move.

He checks back in on me surprised.

I'm sick I say.

And I'm going on like everything I shouldn't be doing like at one of his depositions – too much information: Feel achy, tired - don't have a fever, but – I just I feel awful.

I expect him to pick up on it, but he doesn't.

Just says he's sorry, hopes I feel better, putting his things together, going. He said he's not surprised with how I was thrashing around last night.

How I couldn't sleep.

"Will you be…?"

I let him know I'm fine, then he's gone.

I get up, heat up a cup of cold coffee, call the school. I'm on hold - old phones clunk and click before I reach someone who knows my name. She confirms who I am: "The one who comes in to teach for the arts program. Prose," she says.

"Poetry," I actually correct her like it'll mean anything. "10th grade. Mrs. Bernstein – extracurricular."

What I do, being a poet, yes, "extracurricular." And two and a half years since my last "extracurricular" hand bound collection is wasting away in some corner.

ANNA. *(cont.)* The lady says she'll put a note in her box, I can hear announcements booming over the loudspeaker – she talks over it, louder, "Is that it dear?"

"Yes."

"Yes?"

"Yes, thanks."

I hit the talk button with some kind of force, like that was important.

Microwave beeps - take out the coffee.

Tastes like cardboard and vanilla.

I wonder if Mrs. Bernstein will believe me.

Because I couldn't.

I couldn't go back today.

There's a part of me that thinks I should go back to bed, even though I'm not tired. Look at the clock – 10 AM.

Alone in the big, big house.

And I'm...I'm very nervous. Walking around for hours like someone might be watching, unfocused.

Make lunch, watch shitty TV, chomping Turkey and tomato. I watch until I end up seeing a commercial of a wife sitting on couch eating a sandwich - a pixel doppelganger of mediocrity.

When I turn it off I can see in the screen that I'm, I look a little crazy.

And I'm aware, standing there, that there's two people in me: the one who dreamed of Kat last night, who is thinking always of seeing her again, and the woman who eats a Turkey sandwich because she can't go face the other teachers.

I decide to read.

And not poetry, actually sick of it.

I go through my books:
Ayn Rand,
Hawthorne,
Philip K. Dick

I'm obviously schizophrenic.

And, the truth is, I've never read these books.

I just love going to bookstores. Used ones. The smell, the shelves all close together, a winding maze.

I put on my jeans, shirt, suit up and exit quietly, cautiously like an exiled woman, take the train.

No ipod, which I usually put on, no music, just the sound of the train and looking down until we pass outside.

Old sugar factories, the signs, the watchtower, lifted above it all on the bridge.

When I get out at 13th Street, there are people waiting on line for everything, everywhere. Get into my row, an empty corner in the fictional stacks and I can't help but pick up a conversation as I'm rifling.

"It was already dead inside her."

I peek through high school editions of Great Gatsby at two women my age, hushed.

"But to choose to be induced, to give birth knowing it's… "

I stand awkwardly, the women see me. Muttering excuses, getting my purse off the floor, go out in the street, can barely breath –

And it's like nothing I could write. It's beyond epiphany - it's a deep, deep understanding, rising up in me – I've chosen to live in pain - I've thrown away my whole life, living for one night a week, wasted all these moments, days, years when I've always known since the first night I was with her.

I love Kat.

ANNA. *(cont.)* I call her, right on Broadway on my cell, and I can't tell her there, it's too much, I can barely speak.

"I'll meet you."

I'm standing outside, looking down the steps at the tiny lantern lights.

You can tell they're on even during the day.

My hand won't even touch the rail, shaking.

It's so dark already.

I can see her and her papers, against the window.

I want –

But –

I stand there.

Strollers pass me, couples, going, going.

I'm just –

Why? Why?

You asked her to come. She's waiting.

I want - I want to tell her how sorry I am.

To tell her –

I'm here.

I'm here now.

At the window.

Kat –

7. Kat's dream.

KAT. In my dream, I was sitting here, waiting.

How will I know the words?

How could two girls who were never girls, never knew how to be happy, learn to be happy.

God.

Can I?

Can I be happy?

I have no words for this.

I have no experience.

I know how to work, live in the routine of loneliness, how to lie to myself, as if I could recognize the signs and symbols in my own life that I ignore.

But if I admit the dream is what I remember.

It's then.

I can hear her call my name.

I smell something strange.

A warning.

The smell - like cabbage, rotten eggs.

And I realize it's all around us,

A deafening sound.

The air ignited, caught on fire.

Glass, wood, marble splintering.

Walls thrown out,

Roof crumbling,

The whole building is coming down on us

The woman in the coat

The waitress

The kid

The cook

Anna

KAT. *(cont.)* Flames rolling through and over us like a wave to the shore.

Light.

Burning through me.

Exploding.

Exploding into us, and out.

Everything upside down.

Broken.

Gone.

Nobody left.

Nothing but…waiting.

You know when you feel someone else is there.

As if …

And even though I can't feel now, I can, I can still - in my body right before – how – how she called my name.

Waved, smiled.

Opened the door.

Stayed.

Until the morning.

(Blackout)

END OF PLAY

A NOTE ABOUT STAGING

While the action of what each character is doing is indicated by the tile of each monologue, in the New York production, there were no props used and the actors used the monologue titles for motivation rather than literally acting them out. It's possible to also project the titles if desired. Tension was created was keeping all the characters visible and present in the space at the same time even when silent. This way characters can also refer to one another when they speak about each other. As with *Birthday*, each production should feel free to do what works best for them.

ABOUT THE PLAYWRIGHT

CRYSTAL SKILLMAN is a Brooklyn-based playwright. She is the author of *Cut* (directed by Meg Sturiano for The Management/Horse Trade) as well as *The Vigil or The Guided Cradle* (directed by John Hurley for Impetuous Theater Group at the Brick Theater), the winner of the 2010 New York Innovative Theatre Award for Outstanding Full-Length Script. Upcoming plays include: *Geek, Another Kind of Love, Sex and Death in London, The Sleeping World, 4 Edges,* and *Flow*. Her plays for the Obie Award-winning Vampire Cowboys Theater Company include the comedies *Killer High* with director Hope Cartelli and *Hack! an I.T. Spaghetti Western* with director John Hurley.

She has been honored to develop her plays with theatres such as Lincoln Center, New Georges, Rattlestick, the Working Theater, York Theater, the Side Project, Music Theatre Company, MCC Theater Playwrights Coalition, the E.S.T/Sloan Project and to have her work also published in *Plays & Playwrights* (Smith & Kraus) and *Out of Time and Place*, an anthology featuring alumni writers from The Women's Project Lab.

Nobody and *Birthday* were both originally written for Rising Phoenix Rep (and director Daniel Talbott) as was her first play for the company, *The Telling Trilogy*. She's been so happy to see *Birthday* go on to live in London with Sharon Willem's production at Waterloo East, and now the Camden Fringe. The Side Project (under Artistic Director Adam Webster) will also be staging both *Nobody* and *Birthday*, making the plays debut in Chicago.

You can learn more about her work at: https://profiles.google.com/crystalskillman/about

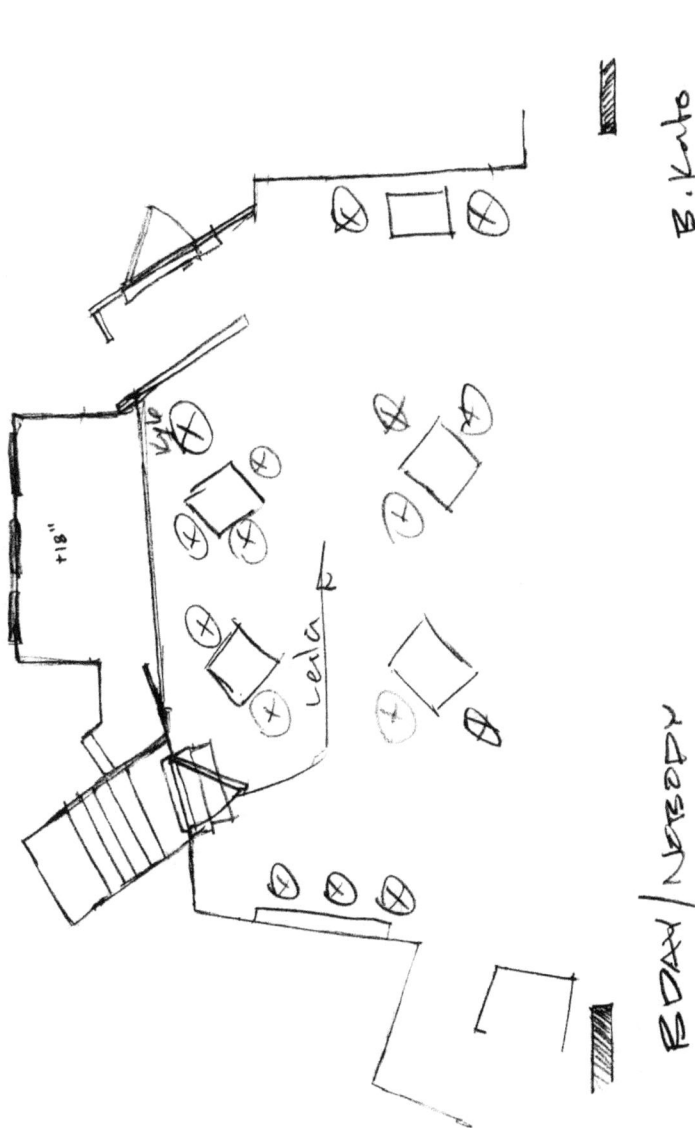

BREAKFAST/NOBODY
by Crystal Skillman

B. Kato

BENT WOOD CHAIRS

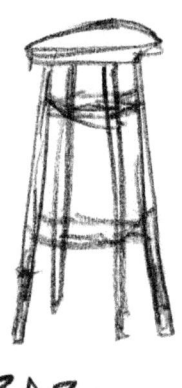

BAR STOOL (WOOD)

CAFE TABLE (WOOD TOP)

OTHER TITLES AVAILABLE FROM SAMUEL FRENCH

THE AMISH PROJECT

Jessica Dickey

Drama / 1f

The Amish Project is a fictional exploration of the Nickel Mines schoolhouse shooting in an Amish community, and the path of forgiveness and compassion forged in its wake.

The Amish Project made its original debut at the New York International Fringe Festival in the summer of 2008 and instantly generated buzz in the theatre community. The Amish Project went on to a workshop production at the Cherry Lane Theatre in New York City, and on June 10th, 2009, officially opened Off-Broadway at Rattlestick Playwrights Theater to rave reviews — due to its success, the run was extended.

" Extraordinary…compelling…the play is also a remarkable piece of writing."
– *The New York Times*

"*The Amish Project* is thought-provoking, compelling theatre…"
– *NYTheatre.com*

"(Dickey's) craft made me weep. The virtuosic writer-performer acts her bonnet off."
– *Time Out New York*

SAMUELFRENCH.COM

OTHER TITLES AVAILABLE FROM SAMUEL FRENCH

MILK

Emily DeVoti

Dramatic Comedy / 3m, 3f

Rural New England, just before Reagan's second term. Meg and Ben are a creditor away from losing their family farm. To the rescue flies a high-powered businessman – in a private chopper no less – offering a tidy sum for a taste of farm life and the pure, raw milk that goes with it. Even before locavores roamed the earth, "back to the land" was hardly as simple as its promise; livestock and humans aren't known for behaving as expected. And so it is *Milk*, an elegant parable of change set on the cusp of a shifting American landscape.

"There is an engagingly original streak running through her writing… [DeVoti] fills Milk with interesting details (lots of cow knowledge) and unexpected touches."
–*The New York Times*

SAMUELFRENCH.COM

www.ingramcontent.com/pod-product-compliance
Lightning Source LLC
Chambersburg PA
CBHW070649300426
44111CB00013B/2335